SPIRIT OF

NORWICH
CATHEDRAL

**DANIEL TINK &
STEPHEN BROWNING**

First published in Great Britain in 2010

British Library Cataloguing-in-Publication Data
A CIP record for this title is available from the British Library

ISBN 978 0 85710 027 6

PiXZ Books
Halsgrove House, Ryelands Industrial Estate,
Bagley Road, Wellington, Somerset TA21 9PZ
Tel: 01823 653777
Fax: 01823 216796
email: sales@halsgrove.com

An imprint of Halstar Ltd, part of the Halsgrove group of companies
Information on all Halsgrove titles is available at: www.halsgrove.com

Printed and bound in China by Toppan Leefung Printing Ltd

The Skeleton. This early seventeenth century memorial reads:
'All ye that do this place pass bye/Remember death for you must dye./As you are now even so was I/
And as I am so shall ye be./Thomas Gooding here do staye/Wayting for God's judgement daye.'
Legend has it that Thomas Gooding was buried standing up.

Introduction

The Spirit of Norwich Cathedral is pristine, beautiful and spacious. It can feel particularly compelling if you visit the cathedral when there is no one else about – maybe in the early morning. It seems natural that as one explores this cathedral church, and the eye is drawn to the soaring majesty of the Nave or Presbytery, the mind should also be uplifted; by the same token, everyday frets and concerns seem to find a new, lesser, level.

Everywhere there are reminders of over 900 years of worship, life, love, struggle, devotion and even destruction: memorials to the unique gallery of people who built and cared for the cathedral (axe marks, even a lodged musket ball, of some who tried to destroy it), the world-renowned bosses and misericords, the chapels, the library and the new Hostry to name but some. All these are discussed in the book. In addition, a special section highlights some of the cathedral's fascinating but maybe lesser-known stories and facts.

The text and all photographs are brand new and have been specially commissioned.

The authors and PiXZ Books wish both the long-term resident and those visiting for the first time much joy in experiencing the 'Spirit' of this awe-inspiring and fabulous place.

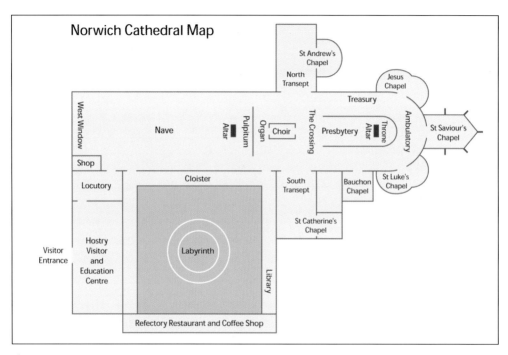

Norwich Cathedral Map

- West Window
- Nave
- Altar
- Pulpitum
- Organ
- Choir
- The Crossing
- Presbytery
- Altar
- Throne
- Ambulatory
- St Saviour's Chapel
- St Andrew's Chapel
- North Transept
- Treasury
- Jesus Chapel
- St Luke's Chapel
- Bauchon Chapel
- South Transept
- St Catherine's Chapel
- Shop
- Locutory
- Cloister
- Labyrinth
- Library
- Visitor Entrance
- Hostry Visitor and Education Centre
- Refectory Restaurant and Coffee Shop

Origins of the Cathedral

Norwich Cathedral, one of the finest architectural and spiritual treasures of Europe, probably started life as an act of penance. Herbert de Losinga, the founder, sought forgiveness from the Pope for the act of simony, having paid nineteen hundred pounds to have himself made Bishop of Thetford at the age of thirty-seven. The Pope granted him absolution provided he moved the bishopric to Norwich and built a cathedral there. The foundation stone was laid in 1096 by Herbert de Losinga himself.

Built partly of Caen stone from France and Barnack stone from Cambridgeshire, the exact financing of the Cathedral is a matter of some conjecture. Probably, the thriving Jewish community in Norwich lent money. Christians were only allowed to donate – not lend – and we know that Herbert gave large sums as did numerous noblemen. Herbert was also empowered to impose a tax on the dwelling houses of ordinary citizens.

Herbert was an enthusiastic and increasingly impatient man and, by the time of his death in AD1119, the eastern end of the cathedral was finished, as was the Bishop's Palace and the dormitory for the Benedictine monks. Rome refused attempts by the monks to make Herbert a saint.

Eborard de Montgomery, who succeeded him, had completed the rest of the cathedral much as we see it today by the time he retired in 1145.

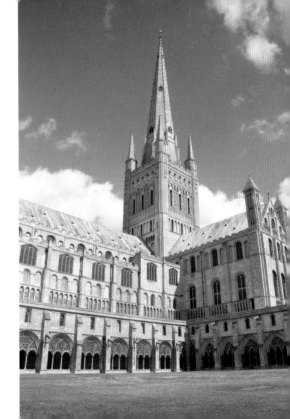

The Nave,
the Choir and
the Presbytery

Many people refer to the Nave as the people's church and the exquisite Choir and Presbytery as the monks' church as this was where the numerous church offices were sung.

Left: Looking towards the West Front on a winter's day

Right: The Nave

The magnificent stained-glass West Window

Nave Sanctuary looking towards the West Window

Altar in the Nave Sanctuary

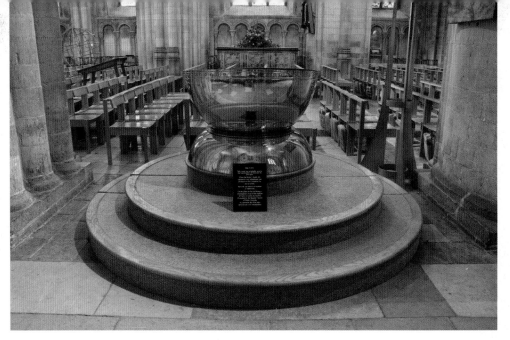

The Font, donated by the, now closed, Rowntree Chocolate Factory

Right: The Peace Globe, in the Nave

Chapel of the Holy Innocents,
located beyond the Pulpitum

Right: The highly detailed
Choir stalls and the organ

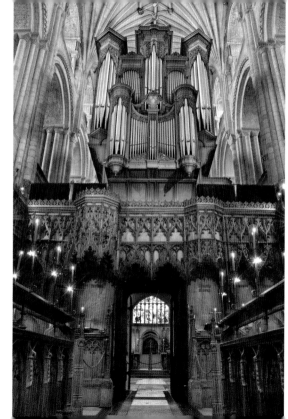

The Pelican Lectern was rediscovered in the Bishop's Garden where it had been buried, probably to escape destruction during the Reformation. It now stands in The Crossing.

16

The resting place of Herbert de Losinga is in the Presbytery, as is the chantry tomb of Bishop Goldwell, minus his nose and scored with numerous axe marks probably dating from 1643 when Puritan hordes desecrated much of the cathedral interior. There is also a rusted musket ball from this period lodged in the side of the tomb.

Right: The Presbytery

Rusted musket ball

Left: Chantry tomb of Bishop Goldwell

In the place of highest honour, at the top of some steps behind the High Altar, are the stone remnants of the ancient throne, the Cathedra, of the bishops of East Anglia probably dating from the eighth century. 'Cathedra' is Greek for 'a thing sat upon' and it is this which bestows upon the church the status of cathedral. The throne has been immaculately restored using medieval oak. Here the bishops would sit. Underneath their feet was a grating, below which would be placed relics of saints which, it was believed, would inspire their thoughts and deliberations.

No one is sure who planned the cathedral but it is possible that the soaring proportions of the Presbytery owe much to the basilica of the Imperial Palace in Trier, Germany.

Right: Beautifully decorated Altar rail which separates the Presbytery and Sanctuary

High Altar and ancient throne

Right: Gaze in awe at the stained-glass windows above the Ambulatory!

Looking up from The Crossing to the base of the Spire

 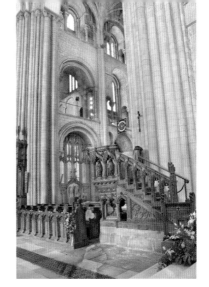

Left: An example of wood carving by master craftsmen

Right: Many have heard the sermons preached in the cathedral over the centuries – from times of terror, such as the Black Death in the fourteenth century, through triumphant announcements like the defeat of the Spanish Armada in 1588, up to modern times when thanks has been given for the safe return of our troops from Afghanistan.

Clock face on the exterior wall
of the South Transept

Left: The South Transept

Tomb of the Hon. John Thomas Pelham DD in the North Transept

Beautiful wooden carving in the Presbytery

Caring for the Fabric

During its 900 years of life, the Cathedral has periodically suffered great damage, sometimes caused by man and at other times by nature. In 1171 there was a disastrous fire; in 1272, following the Tombland Riots, mobs destroyed the original Norman cloisters and slaughtered some of the monks; a ferocious hurricane felled the (then) timber spire in 1362; lightning again destroyed the spire and nave roof in 1463; and many treasures were lost to vengeful Puritans in 1643. Each time, however, determined individuals sought to restore and rebuild, and fortunately later centuries proved more tranquil. Even in peaceful times, though, simple running expenses of such a building are huge – estimated to be at least £3,700 a day.

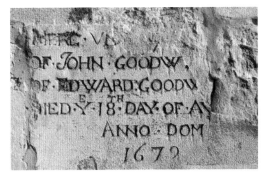

Right: Seventeenth century wall markings in the Cloisters

Today, maintenance work is ever on-going. A second thirty year rolling maintenance programme was initiated in 1994 and this should ensure that future generations can enjoy the glory that is the Cathedral Church of the Holy and Undivided Trinity.

This graffiti from 1634 may be an attempt to place 'IH', 'HI' and 'IA' inside a safe place – obviously a church – in the light of the Great Plague which had first come over on trading ships from the Netherlands in 1599.

The significance of this 'galleon' graffiti image is not known for sure. It may date from the times of the Great Plague – maybe it signifies a wish to sail away to safety.

The Cloisters were at the heart of everyday life for the monks of the Benedictine monastery, not only used as passageways but also a place for study and work.

Detail of artwork on the
walls of the Cloisters

31

The Lavatorium in the Cloisters, used by monks for ritual purification

Details of decorated stonework in the Cloisters

The Bosses

The magnificent roof is constructed using Gothic stone-ribbed vaulting. This required keystones to hold the ribs in place and these were then carved in situ to create the thousand or so roof bosses in the Cathedral. There are more — and easily visible just about your head — in the Cloisters, but these are not keystones. These Norwich bosses are very special because the majority of them, unlike those in other churches and cathedrals, usually tell stories. For instance, in the Nave are 250 bosses telling the then known history of the world from Creation to the Last Judgement.

In the Cloisters are over 100 carvings depicting the Apocalypse. Throughout, it is noticeable that the Kingdom of Heaven bears an uncanny resemblance to Norwich Castle which was, of course, the greatest symbol of earthly power the master-masons would have seen. Of the 128 bosses in the Presbytery, no less than 94 are of various beautiful gold wells, a rebus on the name of Bishop Goldwell, during whose episcopate the roof was constructed. The last to be carved were those in the transepts during the first half of the sixteenth century which tell tales from the life of Christ, remarkable for being almost stone versions of a modern graphic novel: the eye detects small movements and changes in each one as it 'reads' the stories.

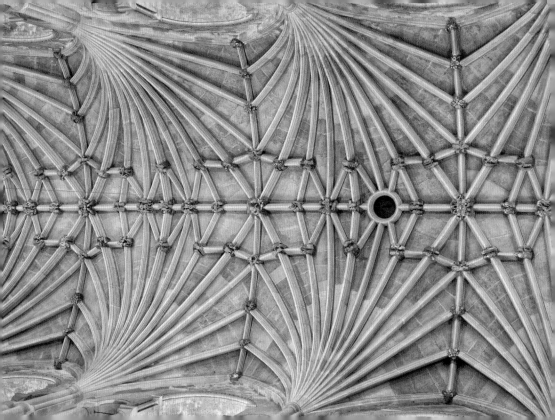

Being high on the roof, the bosses are pristine, having escaped the vandalism of the Puritans and various Norwich mobs over the centuries.

Above: The story of Noah's Ark is just one of many stories detailed in the roof bosses

Left: Roof bosses in the Nave

The Misericords

The Latin name for pity or mercy is 'misericordia'. The Benedictine monks of Norwich Cathedral were expected to stand for hours each day, often starting at 2.30 am, singing the many required church offices. From the thirteenth century, their physical discomfort was eased by a facility by which their seat, when tipped up and closed, nonetheless exposed a ledge upon which they might perch while appearing to stand. This became known as a 'misericord'.

There are 61 richly carved misericords, some dating from the first quarter of the fifteenth century and the majority from the last quarter or slightly thereafter. As a rule, the early ones show conventional subject matter – coats of arms of rich donors; Sir William Wingfield in full armour, standing hand-in-hand with his wife; the Virgin Mary; and dragons, wyverns, lions and bears. The later ones reflect more the follies of man – thus we have a wonderful depiction of gluttony riding on an over-blown sow and lust riding on a stag. We also have Green Men, a griffin, a dog, a monkey, a pig and a fool – all set in scenes reflecting the animal nature of man. It has been suggested that, being out of sight of the bishop, the craftsmen took full advantage to have some fun.

In the Choir are also two contemporary misericord carvings – one symbolizing the University of East Anglia and one showing a goal being dramatically saved at Norwich Football Club as well as the club badge and some of its supporters.

Left:
Norwich City Football Club misericord

The Chapels

A chapel is a holy area set aside for a specific purpose, and Norwich cathedral has six side chapels (four in the Ambulatory). There used to be fourteen and there are still some, now unused, on the first floor.

Walking clockwise, the visitor will first come across St Andrew's Chapel in the North Transept. The name of St Andrew is ubiquitous in Norwich: a fine church, the Halls, a street, residential area, businesses and even the latest car park bear his name. This simple, colourful and elegant chapel dates back to the early 1500s but was extensively restored in 1920.

Right: St Andrew's Chapel

The north chancel leads to the
Jesus Chapel in the Ambulatory:
the Reliquary Arch houses the Treasury

Right: A north chancel window
displays the oldest collection of
medieval glass in the Cathedral

The Jesus Chapel, on the north side of the Ambulatory, once held the tomb of William, murdered boy-saint of Norwich. The top of the altar, of Barnack stone, is a mensa – a container of holy relics. Many are perplexed by the small polished black stone floor memorial which records the birth of Elizabeth Bacon on 13 April 1736 and her death, almost two months previously, on 20 February of that year. This is due to the adoption of the Gregorian calendar which effectively put the clocks back.

Left: Next to the St Luke's Chapel is an effigy considered to be St Felix

Right: The Jesus Chapel

St Saviour's Chapel holds the colours of the Royal Norfolk Regiment. The triptych on the altar comprises some exquisite late medieval paintings.

St Luke's Chapel has also been a parish church since the late sixteenth century and contains a lovely, though badly smashed-about-by-the-Puritans, font. It also displays the priceless Despenser Reredos.

Top left:
St Saviour's Chapel

Top right:
St Luke's Chapel

Right:
The Despenser Reredos

Pause and light a candle in the Ambulatory

In the south aisle is the Bauchon Chapel, once the Consistory Court of the Diocese and now the chapel of the Friends of Norwich Cathedral.

Finally, in the south transept is to be found the beautiful simplicity of St Catherine's Chapel, until the 1980s used as the Sacrist's chambers. It has now been rededicated and is the perfect spot for quiet contemplation and reflection.

Left: The Bauchon Chapel
Below: St Catherine's Chapel

A Few Famous Names

Herbert de Losinga is undeniably the most well-known of the bishops. However, there are some very interesting other beings, some real, some doubtful and one or two absolutely fictional, associated with the Diocese and Cathedral. The first Bishop of Norfolk is reputed to have been a beaver. In AD630 St Felix was sailing in the Wash on his way to bring Christianity to East Anglia when his boat got into trouble. The resident beavers came to his rescue and, in gratitude, he granted the chief beaver Episcopal status before moving on.

Undoubtedly real was William de Burnham who presided with what many see as a culpable degree of ineptitude – he refused to negotiate with the mob at all – over the disastrous riots of 1272. Henry III hanged many and placed the city under administration as a consequence. The present Ethelbert Gate dates from the citizens' act of reparation. Henry Despenser (1370–1406) has a very special place in the story as it was he who bequeathed to the cathedral the priceless Despenser Reredos, now in St Luke's Chapel. He was a very war-like bishop who led the troops that defeated the local Peasants' Revolt in 1381.

Ethelbert Gate, built by the citizens of Norwich

Erpingham Gate is another entrance to the cathedral built around 1420 by Sir Thomas Erpingham, an English Knight who led King Henry V's archers at the Battle of Agincourt in 1415. At the top can be seen a figure of him in prayer, thanking God for having spared his life.

Both Bishop Walter Lyhart (1446–1472) and Bishop James Goldwell (1472–1499) extended the buildings, leaving their personal rebus – carved puns on their names – to be seen for as long as the cathedral stands.

Above the West Door before you enter, is a representation of The Lady Julian. In 1373 she became very ill and witnessed 16 visions of Christ's Passion. She applied to Bishop Despenser to become a recluse and her cell in St Julian's Church is visited today by people from all over the world. Here she wrote *Revelations of Divine Love*, the first book to be written in English by a woman and one which has been in print ever since.

Right: Statues of Lady Julian of Norwich (1342–1416) and
St Benedict (480–527) stand either side of the West Door

Highly dubious is the legend of St William. In 1144 the Jews, much resented because of their business success, were reputed to have lured William, a 12 year old boy, to his death by crucifixion. Miracles were said to occur where he met his death while some claimed to have had dreams about his sainthood and his body was eventually moved to the present Jesus Chapel which became a major attraction for pilgrims for three hundred years. Scholars nowadays attribute this tale more to anti-semitism than fact.

Undoubtedly real was Edith Cavell, who, as a nurse in occupied Belgium during the First World War, established an escape route for wounded Allied soldiers. She was caught, tried entirely in German which she did not speak, and sentenced to be shot in 1915. On the night before her death she famously said that 'patriotism is not enough' as she would willingly have helped soldiers of any nationality. After the war, she was reburied beside the cathedral in a lovely spot called Life's Green, constantly refreshed with flowers by the present generation of Norwich citizens.

Right: The grave of Edith Cavell at
Life's Green beside the Cathedral

Life's Green

Some Interesting Facts

There is a 'Norwich Cathedral Rose' which was created for the 900th Anniversary. It was launched at the Chelsea Flower Show in 1996.

Every 22 July, on the Anniversary of the death of the founder, Herbert de Losinga, an Evensong is sung in the Cathedral Choir.

The 'Friends of Norwich Cathedral' now number over 3000.

The Cathedral Close, extending to over 44 acres, is one of the largest in England. 83 of the properties, many to rent, are either Grade 1 or 2 listed.

Left: Cathedral Close

The Cathedral offers a suggested itinerary for personal pilgrimages.
Group pilgrimages, both day and evening, can also be arranged.

The Cathedral lay in ruins for two decades following terrible
damage inflicted upon it by Puritan mobs in 1643.

The Cathedral hosts a varied year-long programme
of exhibitions, recitals, plays and lectures.
Sometimes the BBC will broadcast from the Cathedral.

Probably to save it from destruction by marauding hordes, someone had the
bright idea of turning the Despenser Reredos (page 42) upside down and using
it as a workman's table. It was rediscovered entirely by accident in 1847.

Left: Cathedral Close at sunrise on a winter's day

The Hostry, funded in part by a grant from the Heritage Lottery Fund, is the largest building project at the Cathedral since its inception 900 years ago. It was designed by Sir Michael Hopkins and has been eleven years in the making.

Above and right: Hostry Visitor and Education Centre

The Cathedral Choir includes 16 boys, aged 7–13, who attend Norwich School and have some of their fees paid by the Cathedral. Girls were introduced into the Choir in 1995 – there are places for 24, aged 11–18.

The Treasury, opened in 1973, is a specially constructed showcase for church plate – some very rare – and is located above the Reliquary Arch in the north aisle of the Presbytery.

The Cathedral tower houses five bells hung in 1463, the largest being 41½ inches in diameter. They no longer 'swing' but are chimed 'dead', and are controlled by an electronic clock.

Norwich Cathedral has had a library – first floor alongside the refectory – since its foundation. It has been plundered and destroyed several times but today boasts some rare works as well as volumes on poetry, history, law and the natural sciences. It has a very peaceful working area for use by the general public.

The Cathedral is 461 ft long, 72 ft wide and 315 ft high (140.5, 22 and 96 metres respectively). The Spire is the second highest in the country, after Salisbury.

Pull's Ferry is a flint building, once used as a medieval watergate. Monks built a canal from the River Wensum to Norwich Cathedral, where stone was transported for building the cathedral.

Left: A closer look at the base of the Spire, shows the strong buttresses rising up from the Nave, Transept and Presbytery. Vertical sections of circular design finish this wonderfully decorated architecture.

Significant Dates

1096	Foundation stone laid by Herbert de Losinga who also founds the Benedictine Priory
1101	Dedication of Cathedral
1119	Herbert de Losinga dies and is buried in front of the High Altar
1121–45	Bishop Eborard de Montgomery completes the Cathedral to the West Door
1272	Cloisters and Cathedral badly damaged in the Tombland Riots
1278	Edward I attends consecration of the Cathedral
1325	Completion of the Ethelbert Gate
1362	Hurricane blows down Spire
1420	The Erpingham Gate built
1463	Nave roof destroyed during lightning storm

1472	Stone vault over Nave completed by Bishop Lyhart
1480	Bishop Goldwell builds Presbytery vault and Spire
1538	Dissolution of Benedictine Priory
1578	Visit to Cathedral by Elizabeth I
1643	Pillaging of Cathedral by Puritans
1650	Great Yarmouth petitions to have the lead and other materials stripped from the Cathedral for more useful purposes such as pier repairs and a new workhouse. Refused.
1847	Rediscovery of Despenser Reredos
1919	Edith Cavell buried at Life's Green
1930	Friends of Norwich Cathedral formed
1942	War damage to roof
1958	Dedication of Royal Norfolk Regimental Chapel
1966–70	Nave outer roof rebuilt
1994	Tower and West Window renovated
1996	Celebration of the 900th Anniversary of the Cathedral
2009	Hostry opens

Norwich Cathedral in all its glory, amongst other famous Norwich landmarks